# APPROXIMATE BODY

# Books by Danielle Pieratti

Poetry
*By the Dogstar*
*The Post, the Cage, the Palisade*
*Fugitives*
*Approximate Body*

Translation
*Transparencies*, by Maria Borio

# APPROXIMATE BODY

## Danielle Pieratti

**Carnegie Mellon University Press**
**Pittsburgh 2023**

# Acknowledgments

My sincere gratitude to the editors of the following journals in which some of these poems first appeared:

*Ambit*: "Morning Swim at Low Tide"
*Cream City Review*: "Ars Poetica"
*Dialogist*: "Rubric for Burying a Hen"
*Long River Review*: "Elegy with Pine Nuts in Its Mouth"
*Meridian*: "A Memory of Snow"
*Mid-American Review*: "Matins"
*New Square*: "Myths"
*Radar Poetry*: "Autumn"
*The Shore*: "Mothers of Boys"
*Typehouse*: "Woman Planting"

Book design by Martina Rethman

Library of Congress Control Number 2022943650
ISBN 978-0-88748-688-3

10  9  8  7  6  5  4  3  2  1

*for L.A.*

# Contents

*I am: what I saw.*

—Clarice Lispector,
*The Passion According to G.H.*

# Myths

| | |
|---|---|
| The sun: | definitely a woman |
| has a hand in it. | |
| A bee: | backwards spear |
| of warrior, | borne backwards. |
| Goodbye ocean: | asleep at your lathe on the back |
| of the world. | |
| Goodbye leaf: | footman hushed and |
| nearing the center. | |
| Lightning: | we *told*. Thunder, too. (And when |
| the snow came, | |
| we praised | the world's pretending.) |
| Forgotten: | return of summer-dry grass, |
| Earth's brow bleached | |
| of color, the poison- | ous white. |
| Birds in flight: | a promise of possible. |
| Fish; their gills, too. | |
| At last, the moon | |
| in her phases: | lady undoing |
| her gown to please us. | |

I

# Matins

We walk that other
country of dry brush
and tire-sewn roads.
Beneath a morning mist
of smoke, the hillside deepens
from camel to black.
I tilt a gate wound round
with yellow flowers
on stripped blond stalks
to attend the white tile
graveyard laced with trees.

Across a field, a yoked
team of long-eared cattle
nears its home of painted
clapboard; two lines of laundry
flag away from the zinc roof,
like kites. My children
crunch a gravel lane to pet
the horse they're entitled to
love for his hips. I might
follow the scrawled cursive
of this barbed wire, knowing
today that if I've loved
anything it has not
been enough.

# Ars Poetica

In late summer parsley we find them:

>But this, too, is a dream I've
>forgotten.

two dry and spring-green
caterpillars, near
sleep, cool harlequins—

>And I don't know the plural
>of *chrysalis*, or why it masquerades

and bring them inside.

>as *pupae*, though I beg
>the internet to keep them, mouthing
>*thesis*, *theses*, the thrill of species on the
>tongue.

Then find more, and more—instar
staged, nail-clipping-wide, easily

>All morning I watch them,

mistaken, flickable, and alive.

All morning we watch them.
And all afternoon.

>and all afternoon, preferring
>a present replete

Trading one glass room
for another, scattering the yard's
choice yields: twigs just so,
and the daily sprig
from the garden, dampened
with tissue and dangled

>with chopsticks,
>fancying *forceps*,

                                          even—
                                          and a surgeon-steady hand.

for their fancy.
When finally the first two choose
the masts they'll sew to,
and ease back into their harnesses,

                                          And even their slightest movement
                                          hints at art

color-matched to the airy juice-box
house I've set aside
to ferry them undisturbed,

                                          though it must be I'm alone
                                          in my fervor to observe mutation
                                          at its most obvious,

you've long since returned
to your Transformers.

                                          or slow, perhaps steeled,
                                          as I am, for the haul.

                                          How odd—

What I've learned:
to expect my own pathetic
urge to occupy, which
means *to let*. Though two'd
survive,

                                          unawares, to dangle, still wet
                                          with birth, and feel,
                                          for the first time, their gentle
                                          fanning, or see it up close:
                                          the slow, liquid
                                          shadow of wings. Indeed,

it was the four I left
inside the day we sprayed
for fleas that, one week later,
either could not writhe
free of their casings, or failed
otherwise to fly.

                        bound as they are

Two I flushed
swiftly down the toilet
half alive, while you watched,

                        to what we know
                        of violence, finally
                        we learn the stakes,

noting only briefly that once,
when I was cupping fireflies,
safety was a thing
I chose to make.

                        like a promise, or a mistake.

# Mothers of Boys

Already the photograph's acrid
with its unknowing.

Your body's a dinghy-sized aperture
scouring the ocean floor, a migrant
that worries the sea.

A boy's body's a sailful of stars.

But the ocean's an unfriendly
keep unmoved by your losing.

And his skin's the color of moon.

And all snow's the color of grieving.

And his fingers are plums whose flesh
you would bloom with your lips.

And his skin's the color of dates.
We just blurry the glass with our breathing.

My hands. What petty substitutes for scars.

# Woman Planting

Of all things
you would covet
more hours of sun
for the garden.

That that vexed
forsythia never raised
her unkempt wiry arms,
dry and budless,
through here.

You might become
this minted swirl
of fingers and fence,
toil and soil-soaked palm.

Instead, slim penance
for killing off bees: dreams
of plastic owls,
savior bats. This morning

finds you again
on your knees
hanging crystals, alarms,
planting catmint
you paid for, this union
you favor unruly
and benign.

Wasn't it you who,
just yesterday, upset
a sparrow's nest
among roses, then
waited behind glass
for its keepers' safe
return, failing to learn
from gardens, birds,
not to touch
what isn't yours
to touch? Later

you photographed
their bodies, thinking
they would live,
that you might watch.

# Rubric for Vanity

You find birdsong
forgettable. Dream snow,

then deny the world
is ending.

You may take to failed
mothering. To loving

in all this green
the highway's song

not unlike the chatter
of leaves.

Your last childhood
proved enough

training in force you were
called to the dock

for de-hooking.
How quickly you sprang

from dinner.
How simply you praise

your restraint
in not sharing the boy

from the city who cast
his line again and again.

# Teaching Commas

That a body might drive into being unaware of its vehicle status

That a voice might imagine its taut brown leather bound by white

Pity we are not sand or water on the yielding where sand meets water

His uncommon blond his windblown hair and flood-ravaged beaches

Meanwhile the teacher composing her thesis on headphones and swagger

Of course you'd spit *mi-cro-ag-gres-sion* as a microaggression

Telling of the child and his tarp it's true I thought as a mother only

*Who doesn't know Bob Dylan?* dimly scoffs a white face from the back

# Morning Swim at Low Tide

Cold water sounding
on skin; metal to ears just
below the surface.

Strung buoys necklace
the rising, liquid breast bright
with gems. On the sand,

a woman retrieves
her wiry dog. Your young son
hums, thumbing his waistband.

A planet unyielding.
Pain of loss: the water retreats
from your body.

II

# Rubric for Deleting Apps

*demonstrably you gave / the world / a fighting chance /*
what else was all / this suburbia for if not a guarantee / you'd come
to cultivate / a living thing /
*swiftly then the lawn endowed / with late crabgrass / the flicker's tight wing /*
only then did you manage / without its constant / hum a theory / of flight
*come across without / binary or thumb*
mindful still of mindfulness / as virtue / hating the chastity / of lists
*what distracts will hurt you / slack squares / dissed myth / pith*

# Elegy with Pine Nuts in Its Mouth

In my mouth the words are first a gag, a memory
of fur. Then, echo of birdsong arriving

through old growth. Is that you, *th*? And where else
have you been, dialect I might have earned, you words

called hatchets, driven and well sprung, tapped,
you sap, you languid, ungrieving daughters?

The way to lose him
wrongly: remember
his dismissal like
the mean dart meant
for you it was.

In its thirty-six months
the cone of the stone pine
matures at six inches long.
Aged and finally dry it flays
open and two firm oblong
seeds loosen from under each
woody leaf with shells streaked
powdery brown. These a child
can easily shake or pick out
with her fingers or gather from
piles along roadsides and break
open with a small flat rock and eat.
Sometimes the seed yields deeper
gold and translucent
and visibly sour. And
sometimes she wields the rock
too hard, learns a vexing
lesson in restraint.

Manifesto in ten
synonyms for nature:
my school skirt after
recess inked brown
with my fingerprints.

Returning then to highways gray as bone      already you unsalt
what water weaned you      no *you* was ever needed by a stone

no light      whether unbraided over pines or screened or floating
out of sight you might have seemed      without a childhood blessed

ballooning taut and floating out of sight      you might have seemed
to wear your eyes intuit hunger      thought between graffitied

overpass and sky some thought      that he conjured cookie wrappers
sometimes drove recklessly      the seriousness of swan dives.

What form becomes
an elegy for him: a sleeve
turned wrong side out
delivering its hand.

I remember the Catacombs
of Priscilla I remember most
of all I remember the tiny
guide in her gray habit
her skin like gold marble her
eyes always lowered her smile
but for the grace of God
and the echo of her slow
liquid voice in eight
languages through tunnels
for miles how it was the kind
of voice I wanted
to chew on and how
her gentle wand
tapping the image of Jesus
in the first-ever portrait
of the Virgin Mary made
a sound like the perfect give
of chalk on a sidewalk and
oh how I longed
to hold it

What I had to learn
from women bound
to rapture by their gods:
how to own my death as I turn
into a tree to escape.

Some strange ubiquitous pined-for fruit
favored by magpies and Aztec gods

for millennia flourished
whether Hindu or Roman now

rests in my seeing the stories-high
*Pigna* that fountain for Isis framed

by peacocks in its Vatican square
or flanked with snakes enduring

crop circles Masonic lodges the Pope's
pinecone staff even Eve, her thrill.

Remember me treed city
where I was:
a daughter, a pocket of
shells leaving, a statue I
photograph too close
for meaning.

# Reconciliation

If I lost so much
time loving fields
instead of trees
it was only for loving
my opposite.

Instead, I missed:
1. the echoes of everything
2. footsteps' various music
3. a sudden wind
   at my neck.

And I don't know why
this place of stone
and leaves reminds
me of you—the reason
I pause nothing
more than the slight
dawn between trees.

Of course I should
have known better
than to count on my face
that day I traveled a long
way to claim you.

Instead I earned:
1. a rock
2. a rock
3. their shadows—

two bodies
joined merely by a point
of view.

Though if I've changed
it's only for want of no
longer caving.

You're surprised but I
take pains to live
this way.

# Pompeii

For a time I became a head
only / a site

of excavation / my blood
on the walk just

a cartoon version
of crisis / the dark

through which we'd
sped / mouthing our penance

to black fields and red lights /
a merciful dark.

Days later / in a shuffle
of blue / parading my lucite

bassinet like a slow float
down the hall / I greeted you.

Born too early too
your infant had

just died. You asked
if I wanted to

see her but / the space
between us / petrified

and I left you / a cavity
of ash / body-sized.

Do you want
to see her / you mouth

of sand / you lead    you
mother    you said / again

# Rubric for Burying a Hen

I.

Your instinct for concern
is developing, but backwards.
Either farmwork or parenthood
has diminished your animal empathy,
though some maternal haunting
may nudge your score
into the proficient range.

Noting lethargy, diarrhea, her growing
tolerance for handling, you fail
to act quickly/need improvement.

Later, you try to forget/make
a joke of/intend to omit how
your daughter may have clocked her
on the head with the roost ramp.

II.

Your disturbance reflex
is proficient. You startle
when only two hens drop
from the hatch by mid-morning.
Then, opening the roost, you note
the head like a carved swan's, recoil
at the thought of her
choosing this corner to die alone.

Additionally, you may leave
the body undisturbed,
not knowing why you raise
the ramp so the others
won't discern her.

III.

Your appetite for grief
barely approaches standard.
When little pressed
you offer flatly to the children
that she died.

You may wait until after noon
to retrieve the body, noting tenderly
the still-supple neck (not bearing
to touch the belly
with its toxic egg) then bag
and hang it from a nail in the garage.

IV.

Your observance of ritual
earns three half stars.
To yourself and the fox
you deny the grace of offering.

Though predictably,
your aesthetic demonstrates
an expert's preference for rehearsed
distraction. You may first
walk gingerly to the creek,
leaning on your shovel, looking
halfheartedly for the tree
carved this year with the names
of your two cats.

After the funeral, perhaps you sit
for minutes on a bench you made
by hand, so convinced are you
of your belonging.

# III

# Letters to a Future Year

One day I'll
summon the pearl
dream of that honeyed
gymnasium where we
gathered in a penlight-
spring to bare arms.

How we sat in tidy
cubicles, patient
as toys.

Till then, old normal's
plodding burn.
If mouths and noses
are real, they're
a summer slipping
into next year.

Remember how
we moved—
arrows through
winter's ordinary dark?

I don't envy
your house's high,
pristine angles.

I think
about stasis—
a new kind of fall
in which, recklessly
sated, I hoard
only what I need.

Above me
the ceiling's
a burden blank
and bearable,

I may forgive
the various ways
I approximate
closure—
lean-in to this
bruise still tender
with what I've not
yet done or made.

I did
appreciate your
fevered vowels,

and this morning's
rain—a blue
instrument I mistake
for adolescence.

But it's grief we're
charged with—
this dogged drizzle,
forecasts nostalgic
with cold.

What future
loss we'll come
to see as irony:
floodlight
on the driveway
passing for snow.

# Autumn

Thunder comes early   and thick, like a theory

vague and wandering,   world-weary, resisting

rain. So we sleep   to the sound of sky

long past daylight,   two dogs dreaming,

and wake to that darkness   weather can wring.

Downstairs, the children   flip channels, all

friendly delirium.   You rally a fire while I

absently browse   for eggs, or butter—

secretly loving   my limits when, late-week,

empty or near-empty   shelves force enterprise;

leftovers rouse   into latkes, or bread

pudding, or sugar pies.   Soon we'll paddle

to the table, a coterie   of cause and effect:

our son nearly managing,   pre-methylphenidate,

the brilliant body   into which he was born

six weeks early, like    a silverfish, spellbound,

his red lips smiling    and raw with worry;

our daughter, a kind    of kindling, insists

on tap shoes; attempts    to towel-whip; torments

yet again the puppy    confined, for her peace,

while in heat. You and I,    some lesson in yielding.

Outside, the hard rain    heaves and drives.

The orchard, warily    organized, brightens.

Sometimes a car    quakes by, but carefully;

at the curb, turkeys pause    and pace, then tighten.

# Of Forms

After the tale of young lovers, I stay
awake, feeling my face

in the dark. Then come into the world
a vessel, bronze and ungirdled

and filled with my faults. A dream:
I wake in a berm,

encounter my own body covered in leaves.
I remember I love

to eat anything
out of a shell. First to secretly loosen

the flesh with the tongue.

# Past Life

*Latitude*

That you like all things

a little. That we could have invented

the blue of this tennis court.

Meanwhile the pool's

ravaged newness undoes peculiar.

I gather my frank evidence

to continue, like a beast who drags

her shadow from a slaughter.

I wonder if we live. If the opposite

of death equals place.

Not a swimmer but a diver—

I'm an axis

cutting water; pity the creature

who lives to surface.

*Homecoming*

The longing to wake

                in a room a woman

has made sparse.

I remember I live

                in the world with my body.

Yesterday walking for hours

                behind

imagined horses, I said,

                *We are in this together.*

What rhymes with upheaval?

                Today it is cloudy, but otherwise

strange; the sun wakes ants.

That's the point.

                One of us is trying to be a nice boy.

*Today*

I don't imagine I

                    have goats and blog about them.

My child falls asleep in my

                    arms while we are dancing.

Once we had a farm.

I try to remember to look up.

                    At least open

my eyes to the sidewalk; the sky is

                    unbearably beautiful

and the blinding pines' furious light.

# Rubric for Inevitability

You may balk when pressed
between speaking and thinking.

You accept an evolving rendition
of compromise, fail

to manage a feminism by which
healing and kneeling aren't kin.

Alternately, you may pen
tomorrow's breakfast in a planner,

dream speakable dreams
in which loving your foil

is an act of self-hatred.
So average you're pulled toward

that clearing of unpeopled
sky, the ocean. In your boat

of self-awareness, with its
ridiculous oars.

# A Memory of Snow

Off-road, half drunk, knee-deep
in ermine he doubled over,

took his fill of liquid
heaves, stalls and kick-starts,

laid him down
in towny white, his fail

a leaden night, then left me
in the gully by the tree line.

First his flare spilled over
the hill, then his sound,

till unfound I stood alone
by the oil spot the engine left.

Above, around, a sonogram
of stars—that quiet, moony

otherworld of clotted almost-light.
Again needing it against me,

I stand tonight
at the dark window

in this winter of dwindling
snow, where snow like an undue gift

returns dampered the bent
world, her body still and tumorless.

# Notes

The book's epigraph comes from *The Passion According to G.H.*, by Clarice Lispector, translated by Idra Novey (New Directions 2012).

"Elegy with Pine Nuts in Its Mouth" takes inspiration from a series of poems in Larry Levis's posthumous work *Elegy* (University of Pittsburgh Press 1997).

I'd like to extend personal thanks to Penelope Pelizzon, Amy Nocton, Kim Kraner, Jason Courtmanche, Peter Constantine, Brian Sneeden, Maria Borio, and Jerry Costanzo, without whose inspiration, support, and/or encouragement this book may not have come to be.

Finally, my deepest thanks to the family and friends who sustain me, especially Matthew Yelland, Marcia Pieratti, Kristin Baber, Alli Noonan, and the many, many colleagues who bring joy and inspiration to the daily work of teaching and writing: your contributions mean more than you know.